Baby Albino Rhino

Written and Illustrated by
Charles J. Ward Jr.

©2018 by Charles J. Ward Jr.

All rights reserved. No part of this book may be reproduced in any form, by any electronic means, including information storage and retrieval systems, without permission in writing, except by a reviewer who may quote brief passages in a review. This publication is designed to provide accurate and authoritative information in regard to the subject matter covered.

The art work was created by using pen and ink drawings, colored pencils, acrylic paint, in combination with original photographs. All concepts, story, composition, book design and illustrations were created by

Charles J. Ward Jr.

Special thanks to the editors,

Jillanne Michell and Mr. Peter Anderson,

English Professors at Umpqua Community College.

And thank you to John and Judy Waller for scanning, editorial, and composition services.

I also want to thank my wife and children for encouraging me to finish this book.

It was a brand new day for Baby Albino Rhino. Mommy rhinoceros told Baby Albino Rhino that they were White Rhinos. She told Albino that other kinds of rhinoceros roamed the world like the Indian Rhino, the Sumatran and the Java Rhino, and the Black Rhino.

She told Baby Albino Rhino that the Indian Rhino lives in India and Nepal in the Himalayas mountain range. The Indian Rhinos have only one horn that they use for digging up the ground for food. Their skin is like armor plates that help protect them.

The Sumatran Rhino is the smallest rhinoceros. It is also known as the hairy rhinoceros. Sumatran Rhinos are from Asia. They are the most vocal. They even make sounds like a whistle blowing.

The Black Rhinoceros can run up to 35 miles per hour. They have a top lip that is used like an elephant's trunk. They love to eat climbing vines, prickly branches and even tree bark.

Baby Albino Rhino's mother had made paths over the plains through the tall grass where they ate. Cutting the grass with their big square lips like lawnmowers, then they would go back and eat and eat. Next, Baby Albino Rhino and mother walked through the swaying tall grass along the water's edge and into the water to get a long drink.

Most rhinos sleep during the day when the sun is too hot. Before napping, Baby Albino Rhino always talked to the birds that lived on mommy's back. Learning about other kinds of rhinos was always Baby Albino Rhino's favorite lesson. After a long talk, Baby Albino Rhino quietly drifted off to dreamland.

When they woke up from their nap mother's next lesson was a journey to the mud wallow. They had much fun, but Baby Albino Rhino wished there were more friends to play with.

Many months passed and Baby Albino Rhino began to grow stronger and wiser. Every afternoon before falling asleep, Baby Albino Rhino's favorite lesson was still learning everything about all the other kinds of rhinoceros that lived in the world.

Baby Albino Rhino was dreaming about the mud wallow and could not wait to jump in. Taking one of the wise old birds that helped Baby Albino Rhino's mommy watch over the young rhino, Baby Albino Rhino decided to go play in the mud wallow.

Baby Albino Rhino covered in mud looked just like a rock in the middle of the wallow. The forest around the wallow began to tremble like the thunder of a storm. Terrified Baby Albino Rhino stood frozen and watched as an armor-plated, one-horned Indian Rhinoceros crashed through to the edge of the wallow.

The baby Indian Rhinos began to jump in the mud, playing just like Baby Albino Rhino. Their mother began eating the many kinds of water plants from around the wallow.

Baby Albino Rhino lost track of time and before long mother Indian Rhino was calling her babies to follow her. Baby Albino Rhino decided to freeze pretending to be a mud rock again.

From the outer side of the mud wallow, a family of small hairy rhinos stood at the edge. They looked very hungry and began eating leaves and tree branches.

The new visitors told Baby Albino Rhino they were Sumatran Rhinos from Asia. They told Baby Albino Rhino that they used to have other rhino cousins from Asia called the Java Rhinoceros, but they had not seen them for a long time. After they played, Baby Albino Rhino said goodbye and again pretended to be a mud rock.

The ground shook. From another direction a Black Rhinoceros family appeared.

Before Baby Albino Rhino knew it, the baby Black Rhinos jumped in and began talking and playing with Baby Albino Rhino. Baby Albino Rhino had so much fun learning with new friends. Mother Black Rhino then called her babies to follow. The baby Black Rhinos shared smiles with Baby Albino Rhino as they walked away.

The walk to where Baby Albino Rhino's mommy was sleeping wasn't far. One of the birds that helped Baby Albino Rhino's mommy reminded Baby Albino Rhino that it was time to return. On the walk back, Baby Albino Rhino thought about how each rhinoceros family was unique, but also similar. Baby Albino Rhino had lots of fun on the adventure.

When Baby Albino Rhino woke up later that afternoon, it wasn't clear whether the experience had been a dream. All the rhinoceros of the world playing, learning, sharing together. A feeling of joy and happiness flowed over Baby Albino Rhino. Baby Albino Rhino's mommy asked, "How did you get so muddy?" and Baby Albino Rhino smiled.

About the Author

Charles J. Ward Jr. is an American artist, author, and musical composer. He completed his graduate work in Graphic Design at Temple University in Philadelphia, applying his knowledge in the disciplines of Art and Occupational therapies. In the psychiatric milieu, he developed treatment plans for adolescents utilizing new age concepts, specifically audio and visual guided imagery. In later years, he became a stay-at-home dad applying his artistic skills to developing the dreams and passions of his three children.

His youngest child is the Hollywood recording artist ZZWard.

www.ingramcontent.com/pod-product-compliance
Lightning Source LLC
Chambersburg PA
CBHW050855010526
44118CB00004BA/169